KISSES
FROM A
STRAIGHT
RAZOR

POEMS BY
**Todd
Cirillo**

Epic Rites Press publications are distributed worldwide by Tree
Killer Ink. For more information about Kisses From A Straight
Razor (and other books and publications from Epic Rites Press)
please visit the Epic Rites website at www.epicrites.org.

Epic Rites: any press is only as "small" as its thinking.

Variations of many of these poems have previously appeared in:

The Rye Whiskey Review, Under the Bleachers, Three for the Road, The Gasconade Review: Storm A'Comin!, Midnight Lane Boutique, Cajun Mutt Press, Black Shamrock Magazine, Heroin Love Songs, Asylum Floor, Escape Is At Hand, Sexy Devils

Contents

An Original Voice

When this manuscript came into my hands, I was immediately reminded of what I found charming about Todd Cirillo's poetry. It is so unpretentious and so understandable. Doors open into a world of everyday human relationships that nevertheless can confound us. This collection of poems makes me want to accompany the poet throughout his days to see just how he interacts with those around him. It is poetry with a deeply humane touch. One may not see this at first, but this is what intrigues me. Todd takes us to lunch, listens to pop music, lies in the bed at his new house and tells us of the train rumbling past. He follows wit, as in this line from his poem, Werewolves of New Orleans, "at exactly midnight/ I'll go outside/ howl at the moon/ let the new neighbors know/ they've got something real special/ on their hands."

Cirillo is rollicking and playful, while demonstrating a great facility with words. I can see the poet in the rain, I can hear him wondering what woman will come to him next, and I can certainly understand when he is confused if a woman is maybe a friend, a lover, or a memory. What is celebrated is this wide-open Poetry. I believe he has learned from the likes of Charles Bukowski and some of his own contemporary spoken word crowd, but Todd's voice is original. His poems carry humor in all its subtlety and sometimes brazen nuances. This poet wants you to chuckle and smile. Read and be happy.

—Neeli Cherkovski, poet, memoirist
   author of *Bukowski: A Life, Whitman's Wild Children*

KISSES
FROM A
STRAIGHT
RAZOR

POEMS BY
Todd
Cirillo

The Most Difficult Move

Two hands
trying
to find
each
other
for the
first
time.

Gifts

The son of a bitch
left me broke and
blacked out
with a stripper's name
written in black sharpie
on my forearm,
three bright orange
traffic cones
in my bedroom
and a two-day hangover.

He is the best friend
ever.

Mile High Club

The stewardess
gave me
her number
as the plane
was taking off.

I smiled and thought
if this plane goes down—
our first date
would be quick
but definitely
a sure thing.

Modern Love

It appeared on my phone,
a brief but direct notification,
someone likes me.
I opened the app
to see who it was.
I looked at her pics,
read her profile—
she likes snorkeling,
kayaking, hammocks
and doesn't have any kids.
I continued to scroll down,
feeling good,
thinking;
I like snorkeling and kayaking,
own a hammock
and have no kids.
I could feel my heart
do that thing it does
when excited,
not stop beating
but a definite skip.
Anticipation was building
like when you get
the first two numbers
on a lottery ticket.
I scrolled some more.
At the very bottom,
saving the best for last,
she wrote,
"no crazy exes."

Ever the gentleman,
I swiped left.

Picture Perfect

I think back
to that picture we took—
after.
Lying on the bed,
only a sheet
pulled up to your breasts
in a redwood cabin
on the Mendocino coast
of California
overlooking the grey and vicious
Pacific Ocean.

You held the camera above us
like a sun
beaming down
capturing everything
we had
and everything
we hoped.

Tonight,
we talk on the phone
1,500 miles and
eight years apart,
remembering intimate moments
of playing catch in the park,
road trips at high speed
or the time we explored a cave
and each other in that cave.

You remarked,
"that fucking was a long time ago."
I responded,
"you are right, that particular fucking
was a long time ago"
and you laughed and laughed.

At the end,
we said goodbye, smiling,
wondering why it didn't work out
but still wishing
it had.

Kisses From A Straight Razor

She offers me
kisses from a straight razor.
She says she wants
to leave her mark.
I don't even have to look
into a mirror
to know
what all the open road sun damage,
scars, smile lines
and backstreet brawls
have done
to this face
it won't be long
until the mind
goes next
so,
what the hell—
it would be nice
to have something
to remember her
by.

The Prisoner

I can still smell you
on my pillowcase,
in the comforter
and sheets.

Thought about
doing laundry
but decided
to keep you
with me
just a little
longer.

On the Way to Work

Today, I simply
want to eat crawfish
outside in the sunshine
with a beautiful woman,
a few beers
and the Gulf Breeze.

Listen to clouds.

I can hear
the punch clock
at the shop
laughing
from here.

Nothing Wasted

I am using the last
of your shampoo.
I spent the 84 cents
left on the desk
where there once stood
a vase with yellow flowers.
I am playing
the Pink Floyd album
you forgot.
I gave the leftover
pack of cigarettes
to the first
homeless person
I saw.

Instead of throwing
it all away
I thought,
why waste it.

There has been enough
of that already.

High School Reunion

At the beach bar
as far south as the road can go,
a song
from my high school years
comes on the jukebox—
"The Heart of the Matter"
by Don Henley.
It played on MTV,
at slow dances,
under bedroom black lights,
on poster plastered walls,
in the front seat of cars,
behind buildings,
at low lit dead ends.

To get this far away,
all these miles,
moments
and years
spent mostly
on barstools
around the world—
a very long, long way
from those dirt road days
living in a hated town
full of rotten apple orchards,
run-down bowling alleys,
an annual peach festival
that everyone talked about year-round,
cornfield drinking,
all those confused first fumblings at love...

only to end up back here again,
fucked up with my loneliness,
sitting on an old wooden barstool
with long gone names carved into it,
in the sunshine and sweet breeze—

just another one of the boys of summer
who tried to get away.

Sucker's Paradise

The blonde is right in front of me,
bringing me drinks,
giving me her number
writing down mine,
it's a smooth exchange
like waves rolling onto the beach
or a thunderstorm in July.
The one in the black dress
loves the same music I do,
travels to the same places,
enjoys the same food,
she says to facebook her.
The redhead says
that she will email me
so we can go drinking.
The one in heels
wears glasses
and says to text her
because she doesn't answer calls
but wants to go camping.
A pierced one wants to get tattoos
and she will just find me.

My social calendar feels packed.

Weeks later,
no calls, no camping,
inbox empty,
friend requests denied

I finally get the message
like a postcard
from sucker's paradise
promising,
"wish you were here."

Smoke Break

Every morning
he is there
leaning over the garbage can
in front of the corner liquor store.
His beer in a brown bag,
his long beard hanging down,
worn out construction boots,
cigarette between
stained and calloused fingers,
on break from the big construction job
on the next block
at Dauphine and Dumaine.
He is back at the garbage can
midday.
Same set up
another brown paper bag.
I wonder if the other guys know
he is gone
for the length of a 16 ounce.
I am never around at the end of the day
but imagine it is the same,
one for the end of work
another for the long drive home.
Work is hard
life may be harder.
He is alone in his thoughts,
maybe in his life too.
So, he works the system
morning, noon and evening
at $2.19 a twist off.
His way of taking

something back
from the odds
that are stacked
against him.
A moment that is
truly his own
and each sip—
a victory.

Beasts Beyond the Bedroom

Some nights
at my new house
I can hear
the train
rolling on the river
at 4:23 a.m.
the horn cuts
through the southern fog
and delta dark
around giant Live Oaks,
Antebellum homes
and histories.
I like watching trains
much better
than just hearing them
and would love to see
that whistle blow through
the southern night,
but here, in this city—
there are wanna-be killers
out there
in the dark,
waiting for their shot
to become
something.
Something bigger and badder
than their Instagram can capture.
The moonlight brings
magic and madness
and it is not
always good.

Instead of seeking out the train
I'll stay here in bed,
open the window,
let the sounds
come to me
behind a gate
that shines under moonlight
and a door
painted red.

I will not make it easy
for them tonight.

A Romantic Gesture

I came across your name
written in cement—
a romantic gesture
of long ago.
A faded time
when hope appeared
as a possibility.

The word
has been
stepped on,
driven over,
puked and pissed on,
until the "e" at the end
is now barely recognizable.

Standing over it
seeing you slowly disappearing
piece by piece,
letter by letter,
it is another crack in the sidewalk
for me
to step over.

Rock Bottom

When you
catch yourself
singing,

You've Lost That Loving Feeling

to
yourself.

Spaghetti and Meatballs in America

I ate lunch at an Italian restaurant today
where the cooks were Black,
the busboys Mexican,
waitresses were blonde, afro'd or dreadlocked;
White, Creole and unknown,
New Orleans jazz played
and the whole place
was run by an Asian family.

The tables were packed
with police, professionals,
firefighters, millennials,
military soldiers,
Cajuns, slackers,
lovers, fishermen,
families,
and one poet.

The food was fantastic.

If 38% of this country
does not believe
that *this* makes America great

then they deserve to go hungry.

Wanting

When I completed
my last poem
and left the stage,
she approached
placed her hand
on my shoulder
made direct eye contact
and said, "I want to see more."

I hope
we are
on the same page
with this one.

Memories

Today in the bar
for lunch,
"At Last" came on
the jukebox.
Etta's voice sounded
familiar, loving
with such power and promise.
I had the feeling
that the DJ
may have played
the song at my wedding.
But, I really could not recall.
I don't know if it was
the Mint Juleps of the day
or the hangover
that hit after the vows.
Then I remembered
that most days
I forget I was ever
married at all—

at last.

The Domino Effect

I went to one of my favorite
lunch spots.
A comfortable place
to sit, eat good food,
read, sometimes write,
escape the fucking
nine to five.

Today, I looked around,
took a seat
at the bar
next to a girl.
Overheard her
tell the bartender
she was waiting
for some friends.
I offered my seat
to allow her
and her friends
to sit together.
She thanked me
but said it wasn't necessary.
I ordered, took out a book
of poems to read.

The first thing I noticed
was the music.
It was
off.
Not the usual playlist
that I enjoy;
Zeppelin, Stones, guitar heavy.

Someone slipped in a 1980's
synthesizer mess,
Duran Duran, *Union of the Snake*,
Miami Vice soundtrack bullshit.

Next, the girl's friends arrived
which included her boyfriend.
They kissed and kissed
and talked and talked endlessly,
each bitching about friends
that were not there.

As I tried to drown them out
the bartender forgot my drink,
the food took extra long to arrive,
when it did, it was bad.
Worst of all,
word came on the news
that Fats Domino died.
It
was
all
off.

Their talk and kissing
led me to think
of my own situation—

eating alone again,
no plans for Friday night,
best friends far away,
face lines getting deeper,

in love with a girl
who doesn't want to love me.

I finished quicker than usual
never got around to the poems,
went back to the nine to five
feeling off.

The whole goddamn thing—
lunch and life
were
just
off.

Protective Measures

The poet shuffled up
to the stage
and set up
a harp to begin
the reading,
removed his shoes,
lit stinky incense,
leaned into the mic
and very softly
yet seriously
mumbled something
about god
talking to him
or maybe
he said his dog

then gestured
first to the floor
then to the ceiling
to the left and right
and finally to us
towards the back.

It seemed he opened
with some sort of prayer
and now
he was asking
if those of us
in the back
of the room
could hear him clearly.

I nodded and gave a thumbs up,
pretending I could.

Werewolves of New Orleans

"I saw a werewolf drinking a Pina Colada
at Trader Vic's, his hair was perfect." —Warren Zevon

In the last ten minutes
before my birthday begins
I sit in my room,
silent.
No music, no booze,
no guests.
Just me
listening
to the air conditioner
hum.
I feel like Warren Zevon
at the end of the world.
There is no special meaning
to it.
I don't feel older.
I don't feel wiser.
I don't feel tired.

Soon,
my phone will light up
with messaged wishes
and I will make each one count
with friends
and bartenders.
Knocking back
each year
with another bottle,
but for now,

at this moment
with four minutes left,
I understand why Warren
wrote *Werewolves of London.*

At exactly midnight,
I'll go outside,
howl at the moon,
let the new neighbors know
they've got something real special
on their hands,
walk up to the all-night bar
on the corner,
order a Piña Colada
and my hair
will be perfect.

Gravitational Force

Even at this moment,
sitting across from you
working on our computers
separately and silently,
I can feel it,
like the tides
reaching for the moon,
an unseen force
pulling me
towards
you.

Once in a Lifetime

The rain
pouring hard.
No umbrella,
no raincoat,
no cover
of any kind.

I run,
zig zag
hop puddles
from truck
to restaurant.

Open the door
everyone looks
my way.
I stand dry
before them—
not a drop on me.

We all smile—
an unlikely victory.

What's In a Name

She is on her way over
and she is late,
just like always.

It has been years
since we've seen each other
and tonight we will drink
and get to know one another
all over again.
Who we are now.

She used to be my…
what?
Friend?
Perhaps in some way
but we rarely hung out
without purpose.

Lover?
That word always feels like
it must be pronounced
LUV-AHHHH
like that SNL sketch
where Will Ferrell
gets Jimmy Fallon to laugh
in the hot tub.

Girlfriend?
That one doesn't quite fit either
because she never wanted me
to be her boyfriend.

Partner?
Maybe, we did create together
but only memories and scars.

Booty call?
Definitely not.

She asked for a bottle of Rose'
so I bought a bottle of Rose'
from France
and it is about time for me
to take it out of the fridge,
open it up,
get this reunion started.

I set out two glasses
and pour the drinks.
She sends a text.

Cancels.

I finish both drinks
and see
exactly

who we are
now.

Dinner Plans

As I walked past their table
our eyes met.
She didn't mean for it to happen
but she needed it to happen.
She needed to look up,
look out, look away—
anywhere else
but at the guy
sitting across from her
stupidly mumbling
with his head down
like a senile donkey
moving the silverware
from the right side
to the left
and drinking a Miller Lite.

I recognized that look
and understand
the space
she is in—
tears creeping up,
hands balling into fists
under the table,
a mixture of disbelief
and disappointment
in the gut.
Another last meal together,
soon the packing will begin,
the lease broken.
Head filled with questions

that may never find answers.

I have had many of those meals myself
in a variety of restaurants
wishing to be any place else.
Inevitably,
a happy love song will play
when
a baby screaming or a jackhammer
would better suit
the moment
and you just wish someone
would turn that fucking song off.

Her tears about to fall,
his may arrive at home
when the silence of reality sets in.

Who thought a restaurant
would be a good idea?

More than likely
another one of his stupid
and uncaring ideas.

I hope she orders big;
a dozen oysters, champagne and steak,
dessert to go
and sticks the dumb fucker
with
the check.

The Funeral

Considering the way they found him,
I said,
"I don't want some priest
coming into my house
and finding me
like that."

She said,
"I don't think
you have to worry about that
unless it's an exorcism."

The Genius of Poetry
(with Wolfgang Carstens)

Sometimes the genius arrives
under the stage light,
or blinking bar sign,
other times,
when she's
walking away—
and occasionally
it comes
late in the evening
with two poets
sitting at a table
of a Studio 6 hotel room
off Main St.,
Kansas City,
no pens, no paper,
only words
between
them.

Title Poem

I ask her,
"Why do you like
the title *Pieces Everywhere*
the best?"

She said,
"I don't know,
it sounds like
it would look pretty."

Finally,
a girl who sees things
my way.

Still Drinking Alone

11:46a.m.
Monday.
Lunch at the Witt's Inn.
I sit at the bar,
the only other customer
orders another
shot of Sambuca
and a Budweiser.
Speaks out loud
to no one particular,
me I guess,
"In the Navy
we drank Ouzo
in Greece.
I was born
in 1958,
there's been
a lot of hard living
between then
and now."

At 11:48a.m.
on a Monday
I believe him.

Knowing

What saddens me most is
knowing
that you're somewhere
out there
not knowing
where I am
either.

Todd the Optimist

Swimming alone
in my pool
on this 101 in the shade
September day
in the deep South,
a slow breeze
off the Mississippi
barely moving leaves,
the music
of the cicadas
rising and falling
in the trees
above me.
I am
completely relaxed,
satisfied
thinking about
all of the
bad decisions
I've yet to make.

The Draft

I am reading your poems
for the first time
in a lifetime.

The words are strong,
solid and clear,
even moving.
Your talent is undeniable.
I turn pages
with The Brian Jonestown Massacre
singing,
"there's a war going on"
in the background.

I read line after line
recognizing streets,
funny dinners, people,
bike rides, broken tents,
picnics, drinks at the beach,
merry-go-rounds, Easter Sundays,
road trips,
walks with no compass,
Mardi Gras parades,
midnight hand holding,
coffee shops,
and heart-shaped candlelight.
I read on and on,
my hand slightly
shaking.

The song
is right,
there is a war going on—
one that I never
intended to start;
a war I've been
drafted into
and now find myself
on the front lines
desperately
fighting against
brutal waves
of tears.

The Coldest Day in New Orleans
—January 18, 2018

The city is shut down
due to ice and frigid cold
but the bars are still open
and hot drinks are served
while the Mississippi flows
unbothered to the Gulf.
We walk arm in arm
to see the frozen sights
of this city.
It is your first time.

Six hours in, at the river,
I say that I love you.
Simple as that.
No matter how complicated
it makes your life
or mine.
It was waiting
to be said,
the words
sitting between us
just beneath my busted ribcage
and your cheating heart
to be cracked open
like a favorite book,
or bottle,
and brought into existence.
The two of us
shivering together
on the coldest day

in New Orleans,
holding the heat tight
between us,
frozen together
in that moment.

A Writer's Exit

I would have
checked out,
disappeared,
ended it all
long ago
but I keep
revising the note.
Over and over
again and again
I change one word
or move sentences around,
wondering whether
to write in present
or past tense,
what is the proper
closing salutation?
Multiple crumbled-up drafts
of one note.
Too vain to leave
anything
less than spectacular.
Always hoping
to gain
some
new fans,
no matter
the cost.

The Weather Channel

Walking away from your place,
all my stuff
in a backpack
and box.
Of all the things
I should be thinking of
I could only focus on how,
you had the weather channel on
as you closed the door
and how I completely
disagree
with their sunny
forecast.

After the Ice is Melted

After the ice is melted
and the tab is paid
I'll go back
to my place,
unlock the gate,
open the dark green door,
turn on the lights,
the ceiling fan
and hear the silence
of nobody home.

In Complete Agreement

She stood me up
on a Sunday.
On Monday
she sent a text
saying she
ended up getting drunk
with an old boyfriend
but she was sorry
and it would never
happen again.

I looked at my phone
in complete agreement
with her
as I
hit
delete.

Midnight Ghosts

All the butterflies I chase
turn to ghosts.
It happens when the music
is extremely loud
or comfortably quiet.
They arrive—
My best friend,
dead years ago
from an accident
I could not stop.
Each and every woman
I have loved
whose heart
I could not make happy.
All those friends
far away or completely lost
that I will never see again
for one reason or another.
The women who loved me
unconditionally but I let go stupidly.
These ghosts come to me
at strange moments
like a drunken dream
when mood and music
are equal.
These are my midnight ghosts
of loss.
Tortured reminders
of the aching emptiness
in my true life.

They remain until
the songs ends
and their ether
begins to fade.
I duct-tape my heart again,
close my eyes and wonder
at the fear most would feel
with the arrival of ghosts,
when my only fear
is that they will stop
arriving
at all.

How Far We've Come

"I only fall in love
with insane and unstable women."

I wrote that line
in 2011.

Yesterday,
the girl I am dating
texted me,
"I need to focus
on me and getting through
the holidays
because
I am a fucking crazy person."

Here I am today,
nine years of therapy,
twelve books of poetry,
hundreds of hope-filled pennies
thrown into fountains,
a thousand wishes wasted
on the first evening stars,
sitting at my computer,
alone
writing
the same love poem
all over again.

The Tiniest Feeling of Them All

It is the tiniest feeling
that catches my attention.
One that does not even register
at first glance.
The smoothest ripple,
barely a bump
on an early morning lake,
the imperceptible sway
of leaves on a large tree,
a single sheet on the clothesline,
a strand of hair
attached to the person
you are paying attention to.

Moon Rocks and Magic

And there we were
floating,
relaxing
in the pool,
warm water
under a southern summer sky
with clouds rolling in
from the tropics
at ten to midnight
telling each other
the kind of stories
we tell
when getting to know someone.
Sharing parts of ourselves
that may or may not be
completely accurate
but sound impressive.
I point out the moon
and talk of moon rocks
and the first female NASA scientist.
We smoke weed
and listen to that sound
water makes when you slowly
push your hand through it
creating tiny waves
and ripples.
This goes on
for hours.
When the moon
makes its way home for the evening,
she does too,

but says
it was magic
and maybe it was
or just one in a million moments
when two people
get as close to love
as possible
without being in love
at all.

The Luckiest Night Ever

When my best friend and I
are together
we drink Pabst Blue Ribbon.
We enjoy the PBR game tremendously
like kids playing kickball.
The game goes like this,
under each bottle cap
is a number and a suit
as in a deck of cards.
The bartender twists the cap off
and offers the drinker
a chance to guess
with the prospect of winning
a free Pabst Blue Ribbon.

On this night
my best friend
guessed the first bottle cap correctly
eight of clubs,
thus celebrating with a free
Pabst Blue Ribbon!
Upon guessing the prize winning beer
he won again!
Ten of hearts.
Two free Pabst Blue Ribbons!
It was as good to us as winning the lottery,
in fact we made plans
to buy lottery tickets
later that night
to keep this lucky streak rolling.

It was a sure thing
we shouted and back slapped.
The bartender told us
she had never seen ANYONE
guess two correctly.
It was the luckiest night ever.

After hours of trying
to double our modest winnings,
continuing to play the PBR game
we woke up hungover and broke
remembering we never got around
to buying the lucky lotto ticket
but shrugged it off
feeling good enough
to let someone else
feel what it's like
to be a winner.

Goodbye Song

I don't want to
write a poem
about you—
but I will.
And it will sound
like David Bowie's
final song.
Audiences
will clap and compliment,
tell me
they love hearing it
and
it will make me
remember
how much
I hated writing it.

TODD CIRILLO is co-founder and editor of Six Ft. Swells Press. He is one of the originators of the After-Hours Poetry movement. Todd's books include *Burning the Evidence*, *Sucker's Paradise*, *Everybody Knows the Dice Are Loaded*, *Still a Party*, *This Troubled Heart*, *Sexy Devils*, along with *ROXY*, *Three For the Road* and *Tonight, You're Coming Home With Us* which he co-authored. His poems have appeared in numerous national and international literary journals, magazines and cocktail napkins everywhere. Todd lives in New Orleans, Louisiana where he seeks out shiny moments and strange wisdom. Check him out at www.toddcirillo.com

Also by Todd Cirillo

Books

- Kisses From A Straight Razor
- Three For The Road (co-author)
- Burning The Evidence
- Sucker's Paradise
- ROXY (co-author)

Chapbooks

- Sexy Devils
- Still A Party
- This Troubled Heart
- Everybody Knows The Dice Are Loaded
- Tonight, You're Coming Home With Us (co-author)
- Early Morning Jukebox Poems

Other Titles by Epic Rites Press:

-My Soul is a Broken Down Valice
by Rob Plath

-Fuzzball
by Ben Newell

-The Memory of Her
by Matt Amott

-Bash the Keys Until They Scream
by Brenton Booth

Epic Rites Press
epicrites.org

Epic Rites Press